MW01061950

The Thinker's Guide to

ANALYTIC THINKING

How to Take Thinking Apart
and What to Look for When You Do

SECOND EDITION

LINDA ELDER and RICHARD PAUL

FOUNDATION FOR CRITICAL THINKING PRESS
TOMALES, CALIFORNIA

Editor: Linda Elder
Graphic Design: Kathy Abney
Proofreading/Editing: Jon Kalagorgevich
Printing Oversight: Rachael Collins

Second edition
Copyright © 2016, 2012, 2010, 2003 Linda Elder and Richard Paul

 Foundation for Critical Thinking Press
707-878-9100
1-800-833-3645
www.criticalthinking.org
cct@criticalthinking.org

Library of Congress Cataloging-in-Publication Data
    Elder, Linda
    The thinker's guide to analytic thinking
    Linda Elder, Richard Paul
    ISBN 10-digit: 0-944583-19-9   13-digit: 978-0-944583-19-7 (alk. paper)
    1. analytic thinking 2. critical thinking 3. theory of analysis 4. logic
    2013957774

Printed in the United States of America.

Contents

Part I: Understanding the Basic Theory of Analysis

This section provides the foundational theory essential to analysis. It delineates the eight basic structures present in all thinking.

Part 2: Getting Started: Some First Steps

This section enumerates the most important foundational moves in analysis.

Part 3: Using Analysis to Figure Out the Logic of Anything

This section provides a range of sample analyses (as well as templates for analysis).

Part 4: Taking Your Understanding to a Deeper Level

This section explains the elements more comprehensively, differentiating skilled from unskilled reasoners.

Why a Guide on Analytic Thinking?

Analysis and evaluation are recognized as crucial skills for all students to master. And for good reason. These skills are required in learning any significant body of content in a non-trivial way. Students are commonly asked to analyze poems, mathematical formulas, biological systems, chapters in textbooks, concepts and ideas, essays, novels, and articles—just to name a few. Yet how many students can explain what analysis requires? How many have a clear conception of how to think it through? Which of our graduates could complete the sentence: "Whenever I am asked to analyze something, I use the following framework:…"

The painful fact is that few students have been taught how to analyze. Hence, when they are asked to analyze something scientific, historical, literary, or mathematical—let alone something ethical, political, or personal—they lack a framework to empower them in the task. They muddle through their assignment with only the vaguest sense of what analysis requires. They have no idea how sound analysis can lead the way to sound evaluation and assessment. Of course, students are not alone. Many adults are similarly confused about analysis and assessment as intellectual processes.

Yet what would we think of an auto mechanic who said, "I'll do my best to fix your car, but frankly I've never understood the parts of the engine," or of a grammarian who said, "Sorry, but I have always been confused about how to identify the parts of speech." Clearly, students should not be asked to do analysis if they do not have a clear model, and the requisite foundations, for the doing of it. Similarly, we should not ask students to engage in assessment if they have no standards upon which to base their assessment. Subjective reaction should not be confused with objective evaluation.

To the extent that students internalize this framework through practice, they put themselves in a much better position to begin to think historically (in their history classes), mathematically (in their math classes), scientifically (in their science classes), and therefore more skillfully (in all of their classes). When this model is internalized, students become better students because they acquire a powerful "system-analyzing-system."

This thinker's guide is a companion to The Miniature Guide to Critical Thinking Concepts and Tools. It supports, and is supported by, all of the other miniature guides in the series. It exemplifies why thinking is best understood and improved when we are able to analyze and assess it EXPLICITLY. The intellectual skills it emphasizes are the same skills needed to reason through the decisions and problems inherent in any and every dimension of human life.

Why the Analysis of Thinking is Important

Everyone thinks; it is our nature to do so. But much of our thinking, left to itself, is biased, distorted, partial, uninformed, or downright prejudiced. Yet the quality of our life and of what we produce, make, or build depends precisely on the quality of our thought. Shoddy thinking is costly, both in money and in quality of life. If we want to think well, we must understand at least the rudiments of thought, the most basic structures out of which all thinking is made. We must learn how to take thinking apart.

All Thinking Is Defined by the Eight Elements That Make It Up

Eight basic structures are present in all thinking: Whenever we think, we think for a purpose within a point of view based on assumptions leading to implications and consequences. We use concepts, ideas and theories to interpret data, facts, and experiences in order to answer questions, solve problems, and resolve issues.

Thinking, then:

- generates purposes

- raises questions

- uses information

- utilizes concepts

- makes inferences

- makes assumptions

- generates implications

- embodies a point of view

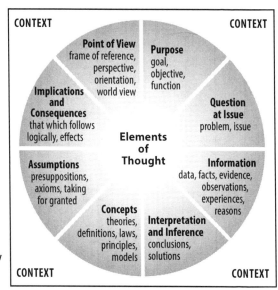

Each of these structures has implications for the others. If you change your purpose or agenda, you change your questions and problems. If you change your questions and problems, you are forced to seek new information and data. If you collect new information and data...

> **Essential Idea:** There are eight structures that define thinking. Learning to analyze thinking requires practice in identifying these structures in use.

All Humans Use Their Thinking To Make Sense of the World

The words *thinking* and *reasoning* are used in everyday life as virtual synonyms. Reasoning, however, has a more formal flavor. This is because it highlights the inference-drawing capacity of the mind.

Reasoning occurs whenever the mind draws conclusions on the basis of reasons. We draw conclusions whenever we make sense of things. The result is that whenever we think, we reason. Usually we are not aware of the full scope of reasoning implicit in our minds.

We begin to reason from the moment we wake up in the morning. We reason when we figure out what to eat for breakfast, what to wear, whether to make certain purchases, whether to go with this or that friend to lunch. We reason as we interpret the oncoming flow of traffic, when we react to the decisions of other drivers, when we speed up or slow down. One can draw conclusions, then, about everyday events or, really, about anything at all: about poems, microbes, people, numbers, historical events, social settings, psychological states, character traits, the past, the present, the future.

By reasoning, then, we mean making sense of something by giving it some meaning in our mind. Virtually all thinking is part of our sense-making activities. We hear scratching at the door and think, "It's the dog." We see dark clouds in the sky and think, "It looks like rain." Some of this activity operates at a subconscious level. For example, all of the sights and sounds about us have meaning for us without our explicitly noticing that they do. Most of our reasoning is unspectacular. Our reasoning tends to become explicit only when someone challenges it and we have to defend it ("Why do you say that Jack is obnoxious? I think he is quite funny"). Throughout life, we form goals or purposes and then figure out how to pursue them. Reasoning is what enables us to come to these decisions using ideas and meanings.

On the surface, reasoning often looks simple, as if it had no component structures. Looked at more closely, however, it implies the ability to engage in a set of interrelated intellectual processes. This thinker's guide is largely focused on making these intellectual processes explicit. It will enable you to better understand what is going on beneath the surface of your thought.

Essential Idea: Reasoning occurs when we draw conclusions based on reasons. We can upgrade the quality of our reasoning when we understand the intellectual processes that underlie reasoning.

To Analyze Thinking We Must Learn to Identify and Question its Elemental Structures

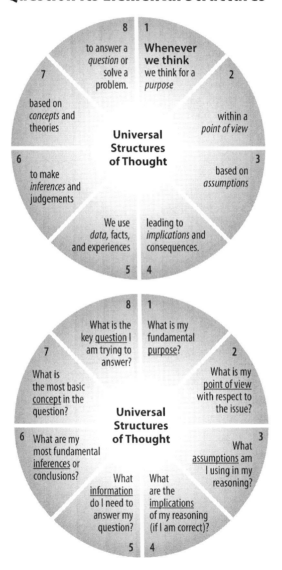

Be aware: When we understand the structures of thought, we ask important questions implied by these structures.

To Evaluate Thinking We Must Understand and Apply Intellectual Standards

Reasonable people judge reasoning by intellectual standards. When you internalize these standards and explicitly use them in your thinking, your thinking becomes more clear, more accurate, more precise, more relevant, deeper, broader and more fair. You should note that we focus here on a selection of standards. Among others are credibility, sufficiency, reliability, and practicality. The questions that employ these standards are listed on the following page.

Clarity:
   understandable, the meaning can be grasped

Accuracy:
   free from errors or distortions, true

Precision:
   exact to the necessary level of detail

Relevance:
   relating to the matter at hand

Depth:
   containing complexities and multiple interrelationships

Breadth:
   encompassing multiple viewpoints

Logic:
   the parts make sense together, no contradictions

Significance:
   focusing on the important, not trivial

Fairness:
   justifiable, not self-serving or one-sided

Clarity
Could you elaborate further?
Could you give me an example?
Could you illustrate what you mean?

Accuracy
How could we check on that?
How could we find out if that is true?
How could we verify or test that?

Precision
Could you be more specific?
Could you give me more details?
Could you be more exact?

Relevance
How does that relate to the problem?
How does that bear on the question?
How does that help us with the issue?

Depth
What factors make this a difficult problem?
What are some of the complexities of this question?
What are some of the difficulties we need to deal with?

Breadth
Do we need to look at this from another perspective?
Do we need to consider another point of view?
Do we need to look at this in other ways?

Logic
Does all this make sense together?
Does your first paragraph fit in with your last?
Does what you say follow from the evidence?

Significance
Is this the most important problem to consider?
Is this the central idea to focus on?
Which of these facts are most important?

Fairness
Do I have any vested interest in this issue?
Am I sympathetically representing the viewpoints of others?

35 Dimensions of Critical Thought

A. Affective Dimensions

- thinking independently
- developing insight into egocentricity or sociocentricity
- exercising fairmindedness
- exploring thoughts underlying feelings and feelings underlying thought
- developing intellectual humility and suspending judgment
- developing intellectual courage
- developing intellectual good faith or integrity
- developing intellectual perseverance
- developing confidence in reason

B. Cognitive Dimensions—Macro-Abilities

- refining generalizations and avoiding oversimplifications
- comparing analogous situations: transferring insights to new contexts
- developing one's perspective: creating or exploring beliefs, arguments, or theories
- clarifying issues, conclusions, or beliefs
- clarifying and analyzing the meanings of words or phrases
- developing criteria for evaluation: clarifying values and standards
- evaluating the credibility of sources of information
- questioning deeply: raising and pursuing root or significant questions
- analyzing or evaluating arguments, interpretations, beliefs, or theories
- generating or assessing solutions
- analyzing or evaluating actions or policies
- reading critically: clarifying or critiquing texts
- listening critically: the art of silent dialogue
- making interdisciplinary connections

35 Dimensions of Critical Thought (cont.)

- practicing Socratic discussion: clarifying and questioning beliefs, theories, or perspectives
- reasoning dialogically: comparing perspectives, interpretations, or theories
- reasoning dialectically: evaluating perspectives, interpretations, or theories

C. Cognitive Dimensions—Micro-Skills

- comparing and contrasting ideals with actual practice
- thinking precisely about thinking: using critical vocabulary
- noting significant similarities and differences
- examining or evaluating assumptions for justifiability
- distinguishing relevant from irrelevant facts
- making plausible inferences, predictions, or interpretations
- giving reasons and evaluating evidence and alleged facts
- recognizing contradictions
- exploring logical implications and consequences

Be aware: It is important to realize that the affective dimensions of critical thought, as well as both the micro and macro abilities, can be expanded in multiple directions. For instance we might easily add the following micro-skills to our list:
- clarifying purposes
- checking purposes for consistency and fairness
- stating the question clearly and precisely
- formulating the question in multiple ways to target different aspects of the issue

A Checklist for Reasoning

1) **All reasoning has a PURPOSE.**

   • Take time to state your purpose clearly.

   • Distinguish your purpose from related purposes.

   • Check periodically to be sure you are still on target.

   • Choose significant and realistic purposes.

2) **All reasoning is an attempt to figure something out, to settle some QUESTION, to solve some problem.**

   • State the question at issue clearly and precisely.

   • Express the question in several ways to clarify its meaning and scope.

   • Break the question into sub-questions.

   • Distinguish questions that have definitive answers from those that are a matter of opinion and from those that require consideration of multiple viewpoints.

3) **All reasoning is based on ASSUMPTIONS.**

   • Clearly identify your assumptions and determine whether they are justifiable.

   • Consider how your assumptions are shaping your point of view.

4) **All reasoning is done from some POINT OF VIEW.**

   • Identify your point of view.

   • Seek other points of view and identify their strengths as well as weaknesses.

   • Strive to be fairminded in evaluating all points of view.

A Checklist for Reasoning (cont.)

5) **All reasoning is based on DATA, INFORMATION and EVIDENCE.**

   • Restrict your claims to those supported by the data you have.

   • Search for information that opposes your position as well as information that supports it.

   • Make sure that all information used is clear, accurate and relevant to the question at issue.

   • Make sure you have gathered sufficient information.

6) **All reasoning is expressed through, and shaped by, CONCEPTS and IDEAS.**

   • Identify key concepts and explain them clearly.

   • Consider alternative concepts or alternative definitions of concepts.

   • Make sure you are using concepts with precision.

7) **All reasoning contains INFERENCES or INTERPRETATIONS by which we draw CONCLUSIONS and give meaning to data.**

   • Infer only what the evidence implies.

   • Check inferences for their consistency with each other.

   • Identify assumptions underlying your inferences.

8) **All reasoning leads somewhere or has IMPLICATIONS and CONSEQUENCES.**

   • Trace the implications and consequences that follow from your reasoning.

   • Search for negative as well as positive implications.

   • Consider all possible consequences.

Think About *Purpose*

Your purpose is your goal, your objective, what you are trying to accomplish. We also use the term to include functions, motives, and intentions.

You should be clear about your purpose, and your purpose should be justifiable.

Questions which target purpose:

- What is your, my, their purpose in doing _____?

- What is the objective of this assignment (task, job, experiment, policy, strategy, etc.)?

- Should we question, refine, modify our purpose (goal, objective, etc.)?

- Why did you say…?

- What is your central aim in this line of thought?

- What is the purpose of this meeting (chapter, relationship, action)?

- What is the purpose of education?

- What is the function of this _____ (bodily system, machine, tool, economic policy, plant, ecosystem)?

Be aware: All of what we do is guided by our purposes or goals. We are aware of only some of our goals. When our goals reflect our greed or possessiveness, or such, we deny them as goals. We then describe our actions in such a way as to hide purposes to which we cannot admit.

State the *Question*

The question lays out the problem or issue and guides our thinking. When the question is vague, our thinking will lack clarity and distinctness.

The question should be clear and precise enough to productively guide our thinking.

Questions which target the question:

- What is the question I am trying to answer?

- What important questions are embedded in the issue?

- Is there a better way to put the question?

- Is this question clear? Is it complex?

- I am not sure exactly what question you are asking. Could you explain it?

- The question in my mind is this: How do you see the question?

- What kind of question is this? Historical? Scientific? Ethical? Political? Economic? Or…?

- What important questions does this discipline address?

- What would we have to do to settle this question?

Be aware: Often the real question or problem is hidden or obscure. People resist admitting problems that cast them in a negative light. We need intellectual courage to bring the real problems and issues to the surface.

Gather *Information*

Information includes the facts, data, evidence, or experiences we use to figure things out. It does not necessarily imply accuracy or correctness.

The information you use should be accurate and relevant to the question or issue you are addressing.

Questions which target information:

- What information do I need to answer this question?

- What data are relevant to this problem?

- Do we need to gather more information?

- Is this information relevant to our purpose or goal?

- On what information are you basing that comment?

- What experience convinced you of this? Could your experience be distorted?

- How do we know this information (data, testimony) is accurate?

- Have we left out any important information that we need to consider?

Be aware: Of missing information, especially information that reveals contradictions, hypocrisy, and self-deception on our part. Most people seek only information that supports what they already believe. They ignore or discount the rest. Critical thinking requires intellectual integrity.

Watch Your *Inferences*

Inferences are interpretations or conclusions you come to. Inferring is what the mind does in figuring something out.

Inferences should logically follow from the evidence. Infer no more or less than what is implied in the situation.

Questions you can ask to check your inferences:

- What conclusions am I coming to?

- Is my inference logical?

- Are there other conclusions I should consider?

- Does this interpretation make sense?

- Does our solution necessarily follow from our data?

- How did you reach that conclusion?

- What are you basing your reasoning on?

- Is there an alternative plausible conclusion?

- Given all the facts what is the best possible conclusion?

- How shall we interpret these data?

Be aware: Our conclusions are often distorted by our self-serving interests, which disengage our sense of justice. Make sure that your conclusions are based on all the relevant information and that you haven't excluded information that does not support your preconceptions.

Check Your *Assumptions*

Assumptions are beliefs you take for granted. They usually operate at the subconscious or unconscious level of thought.

Make sure that you are clear about your assumptions and they are justified by sound evidence.

Questions you can ask about your assumptions:

- What am I taking for granted?

- Am I assuming something I shouldn't?

- What assumption is leading me to this conclusion?

- What is… (this policy, strategy, explanation) assuming?

- What exactly do sociologists (historians, mathematicians, etc.) take for granted?

- Why are you assuming…?

- What is being presupposed in this theory?

- What are some important assumptions I make about my roommate, my friends, my parents, my instructors, my country?

Be aware: The root of problems in thinking often lies with false assumptions. Because assumptions are usually unconscious, they often embody prejudices, biases, stereotypes, and one-sided or false beliefs. Practice explicitly identifying assumptions and checking them for justifiability.

Clarify Your *Concepts*

Concepts are ideas, theories, laws, principles, or hypotheses we use in thinking to make sense of things.

Be clear about the concepts you are using and use them justifiably.

Questions you can ask about concepts:

- What idea am I using in my thinking? Is this idea causing problems for me or for others?

- I think this is a good theory, but could you explain it more fully?

- What is the main hypothesis you are using in your reasoning?

- Are you using this term in keeping with established usage?

- What main distinctions should we draw in reasoning through this problem?

- What idea is this author using in his or her thinking?
  Is there a problem with it?

- Can you name and explain some of the basic principles of physics (chemistry, sociology, etc.)?

Be aware: The ways in which we think about the world are determined by our ideas or concepts. Yet these concepts are often twisted in self-serving ways by the mind. We often use concepts to manipulate people or to pursue vested interests. Use language with care, precision, and fairness.

Understand Your *Point of View*

Point of view is literally "the place" from which you view something. It includes what you are looking at and the way you are seeing it.

Your point of view or perspective can easily distort the way you see situations and issues. Make sure you understand the limitations of your point of view and that you fully consider other relevant viewpoints.

Questions you can ask to check your point of view:

- How am I looking at this situation? Is there another way to look at it that I should consider?

- What exactly am I focused on? And how am I seeing it?

- Is my view the only reasonable view? What does my point of view ignore?

- Have you ever considered the way Germans (Japanese, Muslims, South Americans, etc.) view this?

- Which of these possible viewpoints makes the most sense given the situation?

- How often have you studied viewpoints that seriously challenge your personal beliefs?

- What is the point of view of the author of this story?

- Am I having difficulty looking at this situation from a viewpoint with which I disagree?

- Am I uncritically assuming that the point of view of my government is justified?

Be aware: All of reasoning is couched within a point of view. We often fail to consider viewpoints with which we disagree. Why? Because to consider those viewpoints might require us to change our own viewpoint, to give up some beliefs or goals we want to maintain. Realize that one of the hallmarks of the critical thinker is a willingness to enter sympathetically into any and every viewpoint, and then to change one's views when the evidence warrants a change.

Think Through the *Implications*

Implications are claims or truths that logically follow from other claims or truths. Implications follow from thoughts. Consequences follow from actions.

Implications are inherent in your thoughts, whether you see them or not. The best thinkers think through the logical implications in a situation before acting.

Questions you can ask about implications:

- If I decide to do "X", what things might happen?

- If I decide not to do "X", what things might happen?

- What are you implying when you say that?

- What is likely to happen if we do this versus that?

- Are you implying that…?

- How significant are the implications of this decision?

- What, if anything, is implied by the fact that a much higher percentage of poor people are in jail than wealthy people?

Be aware: Thinking through the implications of one's thought prior to acting requires discipline and the ability to think at multiple levels. Every action we take has implications. What is more, we should be aware that once we identify important implications of an act, we should also identify important implications of those implications. Implications are like the concentric circles that radiate outward when a stone is dropped in a pond.

The Figuring Mind

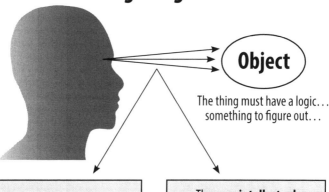

Object

The thing must have a logic...
something to figure out...

There is a logic to figuring something out, to constructing a system of meanings which makes sense of something	There are **intellectual standards** critical thinkers use to assess whether the logic in our mind mirrors the logic of the thing to be understood

The Elements of Thought reveal the logic:

1	An object to be figured out	→ some data or information, some experience of it (the **Empirical Dimension**)
2	Some reason for wanting to figure it out	→ our **Purpose** or **Goal**
3	Some question or problem we want solved	→ our **Question at Issue**
4	Some initial sense of the object (whatever we take for granted)	→ our **Assumptions**
5	Some ideas by which we are making sense of the object	→ the **Conceptual Dimension**
6	Some drawing of conclusions about the object	→ our **Inferences** or interpretations
7	What follows from our interpretation of the object	→ the **Implications** and **Consequences**
8	Some viewpoint from which we conceptualize the object	→ our **Point of View** or **Frame of Reference**

Intellectual Standards include:

Clarity

Precision

Relevance

Accuracy

Depth

Breadth

Logic

Fairness

Figuring Out the Logic Of Things

Critical thinkers have confidence in their ability to figure out the logic of anything they choose. They continually look for order, system and interrelationships. They say "there is a logic to this, and I can figure it out!" For example, consider the logic of love, fear and anger on this and the next two pages:

The Logic of Love

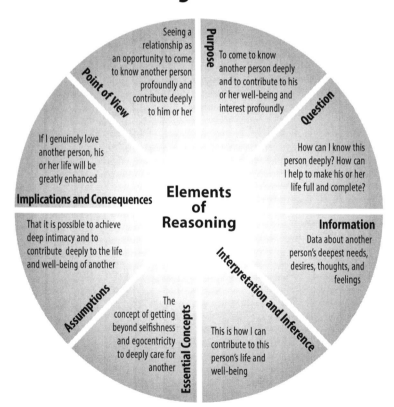

Be aware: Even emotionally powerful states of mind have a logic to them. All emotions have a cognitive content.

The Logic of Fear

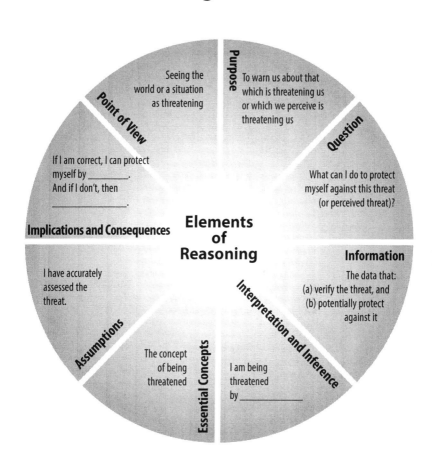

Point of View
Seeing the world or a situation as threatening

Purpose
To warn us about that which is threatening us or which we perceive is threatening us

Question
What can I do to protect myself against this threat (or perceived threat)?

If I am correct, I can protect myself by _____.
And if I don't, then
_____.

Implications and Consequences

Elements of Reasoning

Information
The data that:
(a) verify the threat, and
(b) potentially protect against it

I have accurately assessed the threat.

Assumptions

Interpretation and Inference

Essential Concepts
The concept of being threatened

I am being threatened by _____

Be aware: Understanding the logic of fear is the key to dealing with fear in a reasonable way. Some fears are justified. Some are not.

The Logic of Anger

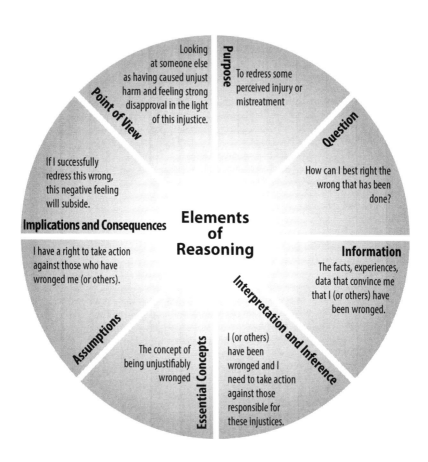

Purpose
To redress some perceived injury or mistreatment

Point of View
Looking at someone else as having caused unjust harm and feeling strong disapproval in the light of this injustice.

Question
How can I best right the wrong that has been done?

Implications and Consequences
If I successfully redress this wrong, this negative feeling will subside.

I have a right to take action against those who have wronged me (or others).

Elements of Reasoning

Information
The facts, experiences, data that convince me that I (or others) have been wronged.

Assumptions

Essential Concepts
The concept of being unjustifiably wronged

Interpretation and Inference
I (or others) have been wronged and I need to take action against those responsible for these injustices.

Be aware: Anger can be intensified or diminished depending on how we cognitively relate to it. It is possible to take charge of our emotions. Emotions are the driving force of human life.

Analyzing Problems

Identify some problem you need to reason through. Then complete the following:

What exactly is the problem? (Study the problem to make clear the kind of problem you are dealing with. Figure out, for example, what sorts of things you are going to have to do to solve it. Distinguish problems over which you have some control from problems over which you have no control. Pay special attention to controversial issues in which it is essential to consider multiple points of view.)

The key question that emerges from the problem is… (State the question as clearly and precisely as you can. Details are very important.)

My purpose in addressing the problem is… (Know exactly what you are after. Make sure you are not operating with a hidden agenda and that your announced and real purposes are the same.)

Actively seek the information most relevant to the question. (Include in that information options for action, both short-term and long-term. Recognize limitations in terms of money, time, and power.)

Some important assumptions I am using in my thinking are… (Figure out what you are taking for granted. Watch out for self-serving or unjustified assumptions.)

If we solve this problem, some important implications are… If we fail to solve this problem, some important implications are… (Evaluate options, taking into account the advantages and disadvantages of possible decisions before acting. What consequences are likely to follow from this or that decision?)

The most important concepts, theories, or ideas I need to use in my thinking are… (Figure out all significant ideas needed to understand and solve the problem. You may need to analyze these concepts. Use a good dictionary.)

The point(s) of view is/are as follows: (Know the point of view from which your thinking begins. Be especially careful to determine whether multiple points of view are relevant.)

After reasoning through the parts of thinking above, the best solution (conclusion) to the problem is… (If the problem involves multiple conflicting points of view, you will have to assess which solution is the best. If the problem is one-dimensional, there may be just one "correct" solution.)

Analyzing Problems
The Problem of Polution as an Example[1]

What is the problem? The problem is pollution and the fact that because people are not doing enough to reduce it, a host of negative consequences are occurring (e.g. increased medical problems, loss of animal and plant life, increased contamination of the earth's water sources).

Questions that emerge from the problem are... What can I personally do to reduce pollution? A related question is: What can we collectively do to reduce pollution?

My purpose in addressing the problem is to increase the things I do to contribute to a more healthy biosphere.

The important information relevant to the question is information about what I am currently doing to increase pollution (such as generating trash that could be recycled, driving a car, etc.), information about what I could do to reduce the amount of pollution I contribute to (such as locating recycling centers, pursuing alternative forms of transportation, etc.), information about environmental groups I might support, etc.

Some important assumptions I am using in my thinking are that pollution is causing significant damage to the biosphere, that everyone can help reduce pollution, that I, and everyone else, have an obligation to make a significant effort to help reduce pollution.

If many people were to reason well through this issue, some implications are that there would be a longer and higher quality of life for millions of people. Additionally, plant and animal species and ecosystems would be protected. A host of other positive implications would follow as well, implications for the atmosphere, the waterways, the forests, etc.

The most important concepts, or ideas, I need to use in my thinking are the concepts of pollution, and that of a healthy biosphere. Each of these concepts leads to a host of further technical, ecological, and ethical concepts required to understand the multiple dimensions of pollution and the ethical responsibilities that knowledge of its many harmful effects entails.

My point of view is as follows: I am looking at pollution. I am seeing it as something I can help reduce through many means.

After reasoning through the parts of thinking above, the best solution (conclusion) to the problem will be to put into action the various options that my research has revealed.

Analyzing the Logic of an Article, Essay or Chapter

One important way to understand an essay, article or chapter is through the analysis of the parts of the author's reasoning. Once you have done this, you can evaluate the author's reasoning using intellectual standards (see page 9). Here is a template to follow:

1)   The main **PURPOSE** of this article is _____.
     (Here you are trying to state, as accurately as possible, the author's intent in writing the article. What was the author trying to accomplish?)

2)   The key **QUESTION** that the author is addressing is _____
     _____.

     (Your goal is to figure out the key question that was in the mind of the author when he/she wrote the article. What was the key question addressed in the article?)

3)   The most important **INFORMATION** in this article is _____
     _____.

     (You want to identify the key information the author used, or presupposed, in the article to support his/her main arguments. Here you are looking for facts, experiences, and/or data the author is using to support his/her conclusions.)

4)   The main **INFERENCES** in this article are _____
     _____.

     (You want to identify the most important conclusions the author comes to and presents in the article).

5)   The key **CONCEPT**(s) we need to understand in this article is (are)
     _____. By these concepts the author means _____
     _____.

     (To identify these ideas, ask yourself: What are the most important ideas that you would have to know to understand the author's line of reasoning? Then briefly elaborate what the author means by these ideas.)

6)   The main **ASSUMPTION**(s) underlying the author's thinking is (are)
     _____.

(Ask yourself: What is the author taking for granted [that might be questioned]? The assumptions are generalizations that the author does not think he/she has to defend in the context of writing the article, and they are usually unstated. This is where the author's thinking logically begins.)

7a) If we accept this line of reasoning (completely or partially), the **IMPLICATIONS** are _____.
(What consequences are likely to follow if people take the author's line of reasoning seriously? Here you are to pursue the logical implications of the author's position. You should include implications that the author states, and also those that the author does not state.)

7b) If we fail to accept this line of reasoning, the **IMPLICATIONS** are _____ _____.
(What consequences are likely to follow if people ignore the author's reasoning?)

8)   The main **POINT(S) OF VIEW** presented in this article is (are) _____ _____.
(The main question you are trying to answer here is: What is the author looking at, and how is he/she seeing it? For example, in this mini-guide we are looking at "analysis" and seeing it "as requiring one to understand" and routinely apply the elements of reasoning when thinking through problems, issues, subjects, etc.).

If you truly understand these structures as they interrelate in an article, essay or chapter, you should be able to empathically role-play the thinking of the author. These are the eight basic structures that define all reasoning. They are the essential elements of thought.

Be aware: It is possible to use the basic structures of thinking to analyze articles, essays, and chapters. This analysis will deepen one's insight into the author's reasoning.

Analyzing the Logic of an Article: An Example

On the next page you will find an analysis of the following brief article (see pages 28–29 for the analysis template).

Is it Possible for the News Media to Reform?[2]

To provide their publics with non-biased writing, journalists around the world, would have to, first, enter empathically into world views to which they are not at present sympathetic. They would have to imagine writing for audiences that hold views antithetical to the ones they hold. They would have to develop insights into their own sociocentrism. They would have to do the things done by critical consumers of the news. The most significant problem is that, were they to do so, their readers would perceive their articles as "biased" and "slanted," as "propaganda." These reporters would be seen as irresponsible, as allowing their personal point of view to bias their journalistic writings. Imagine Israeli journalists writing articles that present the Palestinian point of view sympathetically. Imagine Pakistani journalists writing articles that present the Indian point of view sympathetically.

The most basic point is this: journalists do not determine the nature and demands of their job. They do not determine what their readers want or think or hate or fear. The nature and demands of their job are determined by the broader nature of societies themselves and the beliefs, values and world views of its members. It is human nature to see the world, in the first instance, in egocentric and sociocentric terms. Most people are not interested in having their minds broadened. They want their present beliefs and values extolled and confirmed. Like football fans, they want the home team to win, and when it wins to triumph gloriously. If they lose, they want to be told that the game wasn't important, or that the other side cheated, or that the officials were biased against them.

As long as the overwhelming mass of persons in the broader society are drawn to news articles that reinforce, and do not question, their fundamental views or passions, the economic imperatives will remain the same. The logic is parallel to that of reforming a nation's eating habits. As long as the mass of people want high fat processed foods, the market will sell high fat and processed foods to them. And as long as the mass of people want simplistic news articles that reinforce egocentric and sociocentric thinking, that present the world in sweeping terms of good and evil (with the reader's views and passions treated as good and those of the reader's conceived enemies as evil), the news media will generate such articles for them. The profit and ratings of news sources that routinely reinforce the passions and prejudices of their readers will continue to soar.

---

[2] Paul, R. and Elder, L. (2002). The Guide for Conscientious Citizens on How to Detect Media Bias and Propaganda. Dillon Beach, CA: Foundation for Critical Thinking.

The main purpose of this article is to show why the news media are not likely to alter their traditional practices of slanting the news in keeping with audience preconceptions.

The key question that the author is addressing is: "Why is it not possible for the news media to reform?"

The most important information in this article is:

1. information about how and why the news media currently operates:

   a. that the news media slant stories to fit the viewpoint of their audience. "Most people are not interested in having their views broadened…Like football fans they want the home team to win… The overwhelming mass of persons in the broader society are drawn to news articles that reinforce, and do not question, their fundamental views or passions."

   b. that the fundamental purpose of the mainstream news media is to make money. "As long as the mass of people want simplistic news articles…the news media will generate such articles for them. The profit and ratings of news sources that routinely reinforce the passions and prejudices of their readers will continue to soar."

2. information about how the news media would have to change to be more intellectually responsible:

   a. that the news media would have to actively enter differing world views "Imagine Israeli journalists writing articles that present the Palestinian point of view sympathetically. Imagine Pakistani journalists writing articles that present the Indian point of view sympathetically."

   b. That the news media would have to "develop insights into their own sociocentrism."

The main inferences in this article are: "As long as the overwhelming mass of persons in the broader society are drawn to news articles that reinforce, and do not question, their fundamental views or passions," the news will be presented in a biased way. Because the fundamental purpose of the media is to make money, and the only way people will buy papers is if their sociocentric views are reinforced and not questioned, the media will continue to distort events in accordance with audience views.

The key concepts that guide the author's reasoning in this article are: biased and unbiased journalism, egocentrism and sociocentrism, propaganda. (Each of these concepts should be elaborated.)

The main assumptions underlying the author's thinking are: The driving force behind the news media is vested interest – i.e. making money; that the news media therefore pander to their readers' views so as to sell more papers; but that, at the same time, the news media must appear to function objectively and fairly.

If this line of reasoning is justified, the implications are: Citizens need to think critically about the news media and how they systematically distort stories in accordance with reader bias. They need to notice how their own sociocentric views are intensified by what they read.

The main point of view presented in this article is: The world news media function as profit-making enterprises that structure the news to pander to reader and society prejudices.

Analyzing the Logic of a Textbook

1) The main **PURPOSE** of this textbook is _____.

2) The key **QUESTION**(s) that the author is addressing in the textbook is(are) __
   _____ .

3) The most important kinds of **INFORMATION** in this textbook are_____
   _____ .

4) The main **INFERENCES** (and conclusions) in this textbook are _____
   _____ .

5) The key **CONCEPT**(s) we need to understand in this textbook is(are) _____
   _____ .

   By these concepts the author means_____
   _____ .

6) The main **ASSUMPTION**(s) underlying the author's thinking is(are) _____
   _____ .

7a) If people take the textbook seriously, the **IMPLICATIONS** are _____
   _____ .

7b) If people fail to take the textbook seriously, the **IMPLICATIONS** are _____
   _____ .

8) The main **POINT(S) OF VIEW** presented in this textbook is(are) _____
   _____ .

Be aware: Students who take the time to figure out the logic of their textbooks develop central organizers into which they can integrate all of their learning from those textbooks. Fragmentation and short-term cramming are now fundamental barriers to deep and integrated learning.

Evaluating an Author's Reasoning

1. Identify the author's **PURPOSE**: Is the purpose of the author well-stated or clearly implied? Is it justifiable?

2. Identify the key **QUESTION** which the written piece answers: Is the question at issue well-stated (or clearly implied)? Is it clear and unbiased? Does the expression of the question do justice to the complexity of the matter at issue? Are the question and purpose directly relevant to each other?

3. Identify the most important **INFORMATION** presented by the author: Does the writer cite relevant evidence, experiences, and/or information essential to the issue? Is the information accurate and directly relevant to the question at issue? Does the writer address the complexities of the issue?

4. Identify the most fundamental **CONCEPTS** which are at the heart of the author's reasoning: Does the writer clarify key ideas when necessary? Are the ideas used justifiably?

5. Identify the author's **ASSUMPTIONS**: Does the writer show a sensitivity to what he or she is taking for granted or assuming (insofar as those assumptions might reasonably be questioned)? Or does the writer use questionable assumptions without addressing problems inherent in those assumptions?

6. Identify the most important **INFERENCES** or conclusions in the written piece: Do the inferences and conclusions made by the author clearly follow from the information relevant to the issue, or does the author jump to unjustifiable conclusions? Does the author consider alternative conclusions where the issue is complex? In other words, does the author use a sound line of reasoning to come to logical conclusions, or can you identify flaws in the reasoning somewhere?

7. Identify the author's **POINT OF VIEW**: Does the author show a sensitivity to alternative relevant points of view or lines of reasoning? Does he or she consider and respond to objections framed from other relevant points of view?

8. Identify **IMPLICATIONS**: Does the writer display a sensitivity to the implications and consequences of the position he or she is taking?

Be aware: You can evaluate thinking by applying intellectual standards to its component parts.

Analyzing the Logic of a Subject

When we understand the elements of reasoning, we realize that all subjects, all disciplines, have a fundamental logic defined by the structures of thought embedded in them.

Therefore, to lay bare a subject's most fundamental logic, we should begin with these questions:

- What is the main **PURPOSE** or **GOAL** of studying this subject? What are people in this field trying to accomplish?
- What kinds of **QUESTIONS** do they ask? What kinds of problems do they try to solve?
- What sorts of **INFORMATION** or data do they gather?
- What types of **INFERENCES** or judgments do they typically make? (Judgments about…)
- How do they go about gathering information in ways that are distinctive to this field?
- What are the most basic ideas, **CONCEPTS** or theories in this field?
- What do professionals in this field take for granted or **ASSUME**?
- How should studying this field affect my view of the world?
- What **VIEWPOINT** is fostered in this field?
- What **IMPLICATIONS** follow from studying this discipline? How are the products of this field used in everyday life?

Analyzing the Logic of Instruction

These questions can be contextualized for any given class day, chapter in the textbook and dimension of study. For example, on any given day you might ask one or more of the following questions:

- What is our main **PURPOSE** or **GOAL** today? What are we trying to accomplish?
- What kinds of **QUESTIONS** are we asking? What kinds of problems are we trying to solve? How does this problem relate to everyday life?
- What sort of **INFORMATION** or data do we need? How can we get that information?
- What is the most basic idea, **CONCEPT** or theory we need to understand to solve the problem we are most immediately posing?
- From what **POINT OF VIEW** should we look at this problem?
- What can we safely **ASSUME** as we reason through this problem?
- Should we call into question any of the **INFERENCES** that have been made?
- What are the **IMPLICATIONS** of what we are studying?

The Logic of Science

Purpose
To figure out how the physical world operates through systematic observation and experimentation

Point of View
Looking at the physical world as something to be understood through careful observation and systematic study

Question
What can be figured out about how the physical world operates by observation and experimentation

Implications and Consequences
If we systematically study the physical world, we can gain important knowledge about that world.

Elements of Reasoning

Information
Facts that can be systematically gathered about the physical world

Assumptions
That there are laws at work in the physical world that can be figured out through systematic observation and experimentation

Essential Concepts
The workings of the physical world as predictable and understandable through carefully designed hypotheses, predictions and experimentation

Interpretation and Inference
Judgements based on observations and experimentation that lead to systematized knowledge of nature and the physical world

Be aware: Many people who have studied science in school fail to think scientifically in their professional and personal lives.

The Logic of History

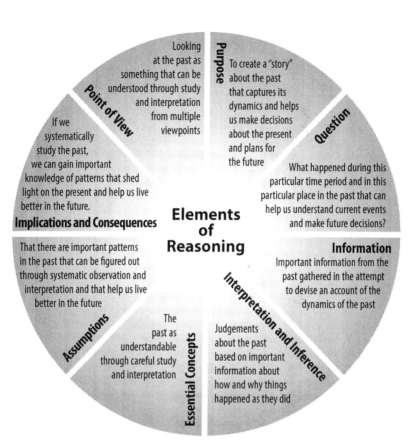

Point of View
Looking at the past as something that can be understood through study and interpretation from multiple viewpoints

Purpose
To create a "story" about the past that captures its dynamics and helps us make decisions about the present and plans for the future

Question
What happened during this particular time period and in this particular place in the past that can help us understand current events and make future decisions?

If we systematically study the past, we can gain important knowledge of patterns that shed light on the present and help us live better in the future.

Implications and Consequences
That there are important patterns in the past that can be figured out through systematic observation and interpretation and that help us live better in the future

Elements of Reasoning

Information
Important information from the past gathered in the attempt to devise an account of the dynamics of the past

Assumptions
The past as understandable through careful study and interpretation

Essential Concepts

Interpretation and Inference
Judgements about the past based on important information about how and why things happened as they did

Be aware: Much human thinking is "historical." We use our beliefs (formed in the past) to make thousands of decisions in the present and plans for the future. Much of this historical thinking is deeply flawed.

The Logic of Sociology

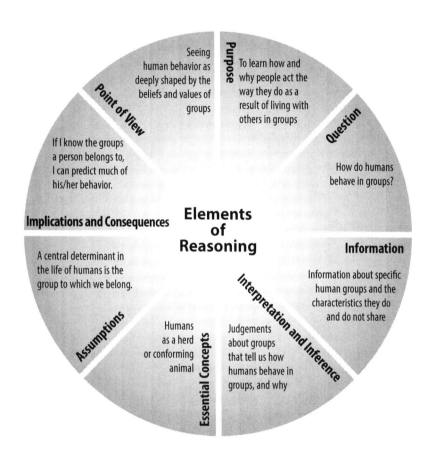

Be aware: Much of our everyday decision-making is based on poor "sociological" thinking. For example, we often uncritically conform to peer groups when we should question them or note their contradictions and inconsistencies.

The Logic of Economics

Purpose:
To develop theories that explain the distribution of goods and services within a society, as well as theories that define how goods and services should be distributed.

Key Questions:
How are goods and services produced, distributed and consumed within any given society? How should they be? What is the best way to determine what people should get and how they should be allowed to get it? For example, to what extent, should people be encouraged to pursue wealth and power principally for their own benefit? To what extent, on the other hand, should society try to provide equal access to education, wealth, and power? What are the strengths and weaknesses of competing economic theories?

Information:
Economists from differing schools of thought disagree on the information they use in reasoning through economic problems. Those who favor capitalism, for example, focus on information about supply of products versus demand, consumer preferences, consumer spending, business investments, and government support of business. In solving economic problems, they emphasize information about how to keep aggregate demand high. Those who favor socialism focus on information that reveals the impact of the distribution of wealth on the well-being of everyone, especially the poor and disadvantaged. Their ideal is to distribute wealth so that resources are made available as equally as possible, taking into account the crucial problem of how to motivate people to contribute to the well-being of others as well as themselves. The information that economists use is ultimately determined by the way they conceptualize ideal economic systems and the questions implied by the economic theories that guide their thinking.

Key Concepts:
Economics is the study of how goods, services and resources are/should be distributed and used within human societies. Leading economic concepts have evolved, especially through the last 200 years. Some of them are: the principle of competition, law of supply and demand, utilitarianism, capitalism, socialism, communism, marxism, exploitation, class conflict between economic strata (especially between workers and employers), private property, free markets, self-interest, psychological variables influencing economic behavior, assumption of scarcity, law of diminishing returns, principles of marginal utility and productivity, aggregate demand, labor theory of value, Malthusian population doctrine, and Keynesian economics.

Assumptions:

By studying the ways and means for distributing goods and services, economic systems can become more stable and more fair to the people who vie for resources within those systems. Beyond this shared assumption, economists' assumptions differ according to their philosophies, values, and theories. Those who favor capitalism assume that humans are fundamentally selfish and that only a system that utilizes the driving force of human selfishness will be realistic. Socialists, in contrast, assume that education can be used to shift the emphasis in human activity from self-aggrandizement to altruism.

Inferences:

Economists make inferences about how best to stabilize and enhance the distribution, production, and use of goods and services. They make these inferences in accordance with their economic philosophies, considering trends and patterns of individual business and government spending, economic health, and distribution of wealth.

Implications:

The implications that economic theories generate vary from theory to theory. Which of the theoretical implications are likely to become actual consequences are a matter of continual debate. The debate focuses on what actual consequences seem to be accounted for by this or that economic theory and what consequences (good or bad) result from variables other than those postulated by a given theory. For example, did the Great Depression of the 1930s result from a deep flaw in capitalist theory, or did it result from a failure to practice the theory thoroughly enough?

Point of View:

Economists look at the distribution of goods and services within a society, along with the distribution of power that distribution entails, as a crucial object of systematic study.

The Logic of Ecology

Goals of Ecologists: Ecologists seek to understand plants and animals as they exist in nature, with emphasis on their interrelationships, interdependence, and interactions with the environment. They work to understand all the influences that combine to produce and modify an animal or given plant, and thus to account for its existence and peculiarities within its habitat.

Questions that Ecologists Ask: How do plants and animals interact? How do animals interact with each other? How do plants and animals depend on one another? How do the varying ecosystems function within themselves? How do they interact with other ecosystems? How are plants and animals affected by environmental influences? How do animals and plants grow, develop, die, and replace themselves? How do plants and animals create balances between each other? What happens when plants and animals become unbalanced?

Information that Ecologists Use: The primary information used by ecologists is gained through observing plants and animals themselves, their interactions, and how they live within their environments. Ecologists note how animals and plants are born, how they reproduce, how they die, how they evolve, and how they are affected by environmental changes. They also use information from other disciplines including chemistry, meteorology and geology.

Judgments that Ecologists Make: Ecologists make judgments about how ecosystems naturally function, about how animals and plants within them function, about why they function as they do. They make judgments about how ecosystems become out of balance and what can be done to bring them back into balance. They make judgments about how natural communities should be grouped and classified.

Concepts that Guide Ecologists' Thinking: One of the most fundamental concepts in ecology is ecosystem, defined as a group of living things that are dependent on one another and living in a particular habitat. Ecologists study how differing ecosystems function. Another key concept in ecology is ecological succession, the natural pattern of change occurring within every ecosystem when natural processes are undisturbed. This pattern includes the birth, development, death, and then replacement of natural communities. Ecologists have grouped communities into larger units called biomes, regions throughout the world classified according to physical features, including temperature, rainfall and type of vegetation. Another fundamental concept in ecology is balance of nature, the natural process of birth, reproduction, eating and being eaten, which keeps animal/plant communities fairly stable. Other key concepts include imbalances, energy, nutrients, population growth, diversity, habitat, competition, predation, parasitism, adaptation, coevolution, succession and climax communities and conservation.

Key Assumptions that Ecologists Make: Patterns exist within animal/plant communities; these communities should be studied and classified; animals and plants often depend on one another and modify one another; and balances must be maintained within ecosystems.

Implications of Ecology: The study of ecology leads to numerous implications for life on Earth. By studying balance of nature, for example, we can see when nature is out of balance, as in the current population explosion. We can see how pesticides, designed to kill pests on farm crops, also lead to the harm of mammals and birds, either directly or indirectly through food webs. We can also learn how over-farming causes erosion and depletion of soil nutrients.

Point of View of Ecologists: Ecologists look at plants and animals and see them functioning in relationship with one another within their habitats, and needing to be in balance for the earth to be healthy and sustainable.

The Logic of Substantive Writing

Purpose: To communicate important concepts, and ideas to a particular audience.

Question: How can I approach my writing so that I clearly communicate my ideas to my target audience?

Information: Information about the assumptions, point of view, and general knowledge of the reader; information about the characteristics of good writing; information relevant to the thesis of my writing; information about how to effectively communicate ideas in writing.

Inferences/ interpretations: Interpretations of the information we gather; conclusions we come to about the reader, about the assumptions the reader may bring to the reading, about the various points of view the readers may bring to the reading, about the background knowledge of the target reader; interpretations about the best ways to approach the content to clearly communicate the key ideas to the reader; interpretations of the information which form the key ideas of the written piece; key conclusions I am trying to communicate to the reader.

Concepts: All the key concepts essential to developing my main points; all the key ideas about how to write well that I use in thinking through my main points and how to express them.

Assumptions: That the ideas I am communicating can be effectively communicated; that there are better and worse ways of communicating these ideas; that if I want to be a good writer I must be committed to writing and rewriting my work; that the ideas I am communicating are worth spending the time to communicate well.

Implications: If I commit myself to effective writing, I can become an effective writer. If I achieve my purpose, I may be able to transform the thinking of the reader.

Point of View: The point of view of a good writer (in other words looking at substantive writing as a complex process that one improves at through discipline and practice); the points of view relevant to the issues in the written piece.

Purpose

All reasoning has a purpose.

Primary intellectual standards: (1) clarity, (2) significance, (3) achievability, (4) consistency, (5) justifiability, (6) fairness

Common problems: (1) unclear, (2) trivial, (3) unrealistic, (4) contradictory, (5) unjustifiable, (6) unfair

Principle: To reason well, you must clearly understand your purpose, and your purpose must be reasonable and fair.

Skilled Reasoners	Unskilled Reasoners	Critical Reflections
take the time to state their purpose clearly.	are often unclear about their central purpose.	Have I made the purpose of my reasoning clear? What exactly am I trying to achieve? Have I stated the purpose in several ways to clarify it?
distinguish it from related purposes.	oscillate between different, sometimes contradictory, purposes.	What different purposes do I have in mind? How do I see them as related? Am I going off in somewhat different directions? How can I reconcile these contradictory purposes?
periodically remind themselves of their purpose to determine whether they are straying from it.	lose track of their fundamental object or goal.	In writing this paper, do I seem to be wandering from my purpose? How do my third and fourth paragraphs relate to my central goal?
adopt realistic purposes and goals.	adopt unrealistic purposes and set unrealistic goals.	Am I trying to accomplish too much in the paper?
choose significant purposes and goals.	adopt trivial purposes and goals as if they were significant.	What is the significance of pursuing this particular purpose? Is there a more significant purpose I should be focused on?
choose goals and purposes consistent with other goals and purposes they have chosen.	inadvertently negate their own purposes. do not monitor their thinking for inconsistent goals.	Does one part of my paper seem to undermine what I am trying to accomplish in another part?
adjust their thinking regularly to their purpose.	do not adjust their thinking regularly to their purpose.	Do I stick to the main issue throughout the paper? Am I acting consistently in pursuit of my purpose?
choose purposes that are fair, considering the desires and rights of others equally with their own desires and rights.	choose purposes that are self-serving at the expense of others' needs and desires.	Do I have a self-serving purpose, which causes me to distort the information to fit that purpose? Am I taking into account the rights and needs of relevant others in pursuing this purpose?

Question at Issue or Central Problem

All reasoning is an attempt to figure something out, to
settle some question, solve some problem.

Primary intellectual standards: (1) clarity and precision, (2) significance, (3) answerability, (4) relevance, (5) depth

Common problems: (1) unclear and imprecise, (2) insignificant, (3) not answerable, (4) irrelevant, (5) superficial

Principle: To settle a question, it must be answerable; you must be clear about it and understand what is needed to adequately answer it. A deep question requires reasoning through its complexities.

Skilled Reasoners	Unskilled Reasoners	Critical Reflections
are clear about the question they are trying to settle.	are often unclear about the question they are asking.	Am I clear about the main question at issue? Am I able to state it precisely?
can re-express a question in a variety of ways.	express questions vaguely and find questions difficult to reformulate for clarity.	Am I able to reformulate my question in several ways to recognize the complexities in it?
can break a question into sub-questions.	are unable to break down the questions they are asking.	Have I broken down the main question into sub-questions to better think through its complexities? What sub-questions are embedded in the main question?
routinely distinguish questions of different types.	confuse questions of different types; thus often respond inappropriately to questions and expect the wrong types of answers from others.	Am I confused about the type of question I am asking? For example: Am I confusing a conceptual question with a factual one? Am I confusing a question of preference with a question requiring reasoned judgment?
distinguish significant from trivial questions.	confuse trivial with important questions.	Am I focusing on superficial questions while significant questions need addressing?
distinguish relevant from irrelevant questions.	confuse irrelevant questions with relevant ones.	Are the questions I'm raising in this paper relevant to the main question at this issue?
are sensitive to the assumptions built into the questions they ask.	often ask loaded questions.	Am I phrasing the question in a loaded way? Am I taking for granted, from the outset, the correctness of my own position?
distinguish questions they can answer from questions they can't.	try to answer questions they are not in a position to answer.	Am I in a position to answer this question? What information would I need before I could answer it?

Information

All reasoning is based on data, information, evidence, experience, research.

Primary intellectual standards: (1) clear, (2) relevant, (3) important, (4) fairly gathered and reported, (5) accurate, (6) adequate, (7) consistently applied

Common problems: (1) unclear, (2) irrelevant, (3) insignficant, (4) biased, (5) inaccurate, (6) insufficient, (7) inconsistently applied

Principle: Reasoning can be only as sound as the information upon which it is based.

Skilled Reasoners	Unskilled Reasoners	Critical Reflections
assert a claim only when they have sufficient evidence to back it up.	assert claims without considering all relevant information.	Is my assertion supported by evidence? Do I have enough evidence to truly support my claim?
can articulate and evaluate the information behind their claims.	don't articulate the information they are using in their reasoning and so do not subject it to rational scrutiny.	Have I been transparent about the information I am using? What standards am I using to evaluate the information? Do I have evidence to support my claim that I haven't clearly articulated?
actively search for information *against* (not just *for*) their own position.	gather only that information that supports their own point of view.	Where is a good place to look for evidence on the opposite side? Have I looked there? Have I honestly considered information that doesn't support my position?
focus on relevant information and disregard what is irrelevant to the question at issue.	do not carefully distinguish between relevant information and irrelevant information.	Are my data relevant to the claim I'm making? Have I failed to consider relevant information?
draw conclusions only to the extent that they are supported by the evidence and sound reasoning.	make inferences that go beyond what the data support.	Does my claim go beyond the evidence I've cited? Have I overgeneralized?
present the evidence clearly and fairly.	distort the data or state it inaccurately.	Is my presentation of the pertinent information clear and coherent? Have I distorted information to (unfairly) support my position?
focus primarily on important information.	focus on trivial rather than important information.	Have I included all the important information? Can I distinguish primary from secondary information? Am I focused on the trivial rather than significant information?

Inference and Interpretation

All reasoning contains inferences from which we draw
conclusions and give meaning to data and situations.

Primary intellectual standards:	(1) clarity, (2) logicality, (3) justifiability, (4) profundity, (5) reasonability, (6) consistency
Common problems:	(1) unclear, (2) illogical, (3) unjustified, (4) superficial, (5) unreasonable, (6) contradictory

Principle: Reasoning can be only as sound as the inferences it makes (or the conclusions it comes to).

Skilled Reasoners	Unskilled Reasoners	Critical Reflections
are clear about the inferences they are making. clearly articulate their inferences.	are often unclear about the inferences they are making. do not clearly articulate their inferences.	Am I clear about the inferences I am making? Have I clearly articulated my conclusions?
usually make inferences that follow from the evidence or reasons presented.	often make inferences that do not follow from the evidence or reasons presented.	Do my conclusions logically follow from the evidence and reasons presented?
often make inferences that are deep rather than superficial.	often make inferences that are superficial.	Are my conclusions superficial, given the problem?
often make inferences or come to conclusions that are reasonable.	often make inferences or come to conclusions that are unreasonable.	Are my conclusions reasonable in context? Are these inferences reasonable given the available information?
make inferences or come to conclusions that are consistent with each other.	often make inferences or come to conclusions that are contradictory.	Do my conclusions in the first part of my analysis seem to contradict my conclusions at the end?
understand the assumptions that lead to their inferences.	do not seek to figure out the assumptions that lead to their inferences.	Is my inference based on a faulty assumption? How would my inference change if I were to base it on a different, more justifiable assumption?

Assumptions

All reasoning is based on assumptions
—beliefs we take for granted.

Primary intellectual standards: (1) clarity, (2) justifiability, (3) consistency

Common problems: (1) unclear, (2) unjustified, (3) contradictory

Principle: Reasoning can be only as sound as the assumptions on which it is based.

Skilled Reasoners	Unskilled Reasoners	Critical Reflections
are clear about the assumptions they make.	are often unclear about their assumptions.	Are my assumptions clear to me? Why precisely am I assuming in this situation? Do I clearly understand what my assumptions are based upon?
make assumptions that are reasonable and justifiable, given the situation and evidence.	often make unjustified or unreasonable assumptions.	Do I make assumptions about the future based on just one experience from the past? Can I really justify what I am taking for granted? Are my assumptions justifiable given the evidence?
make assumptions that are consistent with each other.	make assumptions that are contradictory.	Do the assumptions I made in the first part of my paper contradict the assumptions I am making now?
constantly seek to figure out their assumptions.	ignore their assumptions.	What assumptions am I making in this situation? Are they justifiable? Where did I get these assumptions? Do I need to rework or abandon them?

Concepts and Ideas

All reasoning is expressed through, and
shaped by, concepts and ideas.

Primary intellectual standards: (1) clarity, (2) relevance, (3) depth, (4) accuracy

Common problems: (1) unclear, (2) irrelevant, (3) superficial, (4) inaccurate

Principle: Reasoning can be only as clear, relevant, realistic and deep as the concepts that shape it.

Skilled Reasoners	Unskilled Reasoners	Critical Reflections
are aware of the key concepts and ideas they and others use.	are unaware of the key concepts and ideas they and others use.	What is the main ideas I am using in my thinking? What are the main ideas others are using?
are able to explain the basic implications of the words and phrases they use.	cannot accurately explain basic implications of their words and phrases.	Am I clear about the implications of the words I and others use? For example: Does the word *cunning* have negative implications that the word *clever* lacks?
are able to distinguish special, nonstandard uses of words from standard uses.	are not able to recognize when their use of a word or phrase departs from educated usage.	Where did I get my definition of this central concept? For example: Where did I get my definition of the concept of…? Have I put my unwarranted conclusions into the definition?
are aware of irrelevant concepts and ideas and use concepts and ideas in ways relevant to their functions.	use concepts in ways inappropriate to the subject or issue.	Am I using the concept of "x" appropriately? For instance, am I using the concept of "democracy" appropriately? Or do I mistake it for an economic system like capitalism?
think deeply about the concepts they use.	fail to think deeply about the concepts they use.	Am I thinking deeply enough about this concept? For example, am I thinking deeply about the concept of "cause and effect"? Do I think deeply about my concept of history? Do I see the important of historical thinking to the cultivation of human criticality?

Point of View

All reasoning is done from some point of view.

Primary intellectual standards: (1) flexibility, (2) fairness, (3) clarity, (4) relevance, (5) breadth

Common problems: (1) restricted, (2) biased, (3) unclear, (4) irrelevant, (5) narrow

Principle: To reason well, you must identify the viewpoints relevant to the issue and enter these viewpoints empathetically.

Skilled Reasoners	Unskilled Reasoners	Critical Reflections
keep in mind that people have different points of view, especially on controversial issues.	do not credit alternative reasonable viewpoints.	Have I articulated the point of view from which I am approaching this issue? Have I fully considered opposing points of view?
consistently articulate other points of view and reason from within those points of view to adequately understand them.	cannot see issues from points of view significantly different from their own; cannot reason with empathy from alien points of view.	I may have characterized my own point of view, but have I considered the most significant aspects of the problem from the point of view of relevant others?
seek other viewpoints, especially when the issue is one they believe in passionately.	can sometimes give other points of view when the issue is not emotionally charged but cannot do so for issues they feel strongly about.	Am I presenting X's point of view in an unfair manner? Am I having difficulty appreciating X's viewpoint because I am emotional about this issue?
confine their monological reasoning to problems that are clearly monological.*	confuse multilogical with monological issues; insist that there is only one frame of reference within which a given multilogical question must be decided.	Is the question here monological or multilogical? How can I tell? Am I reasoning as if only one point of view is relevant to this issue when in reality other viewpoints are relevant?
recognize when they are most likely to be prejudiced.	are unaware of their own prejudices.	Is my reasoning prejudiced or biased? Have I prejudged the issue? If so how and why?
approach problems and issues with a richness of vision and an appropriately broad world view.	reason from within inappropriately narrow or superficial perspectives and world views.	Is my approach to this question too narrow? Am I considering other viewpoints so I can adequately address the problem? Do I think broadly enough about important issues?

* Monological problems are ones for which there are definite correct and incorrect answers and definite procedures for getting those answers. In multilogical problems, there are competing schools of thought to be considered.

Implications and Consequences

All reasoning leads somewhere. It has implications
and, when acted upon, has consequences.

Primary intellectual standards: (1) significance, (2) logicality, (3) clarity, (4) completeness

Common problems: (1) unimportant, (2) unrealistic, (3) unclear, (4) incomplete

Principle: To reason well through an issue, you must think through the implications that follow from your reasoning. You must think through the consequences likely to follow from the decisions you make (before you make them).

Skilled Reasoners	Unskilled Reasoners	Critical Reflections
trace out the significant potential implications and consequences of their reasoning.	trace out few or none of the implications and consequences of holding a position or making a decision.	Did I spell out all the significant consequences of the action I am advocating? If I were to take this course of action, what other consequences might follow that I haven't considered?
clearly and precisely articulate the implications and possible consequences.	are unclear and imprecise in the possible consequences they articulate.	Have I delineated clearly and precisely the consequences likely to follow from my chosen action?
search for potentially negative as well as potentially positive consequences.	trace out only the consequences they had in mind at the beginning, either positive or negative, but usually not both.	I may have done a good job of spelling out some positive implications of the decision I am about to make, but what are some of the possible negative implications or consequences?
anticipate the likelihood of unexpected negative and positive implications.	are surprised when their decisions have unexpected consequences.	If I make this decision, what are some possible unexpected implications? What are some variables out of my control that might lead to negative consequences?

Distinguishing Between
Inferences and Assumptions

It is important to distinguish between an inference and an assumption. These two parts of thinking are easily confused with one another. An inference is a step of the mind, by which one concludes that something is true based on something else being true, or appearing true. Inferences can be justified or unjustified. All inferences are based on assumptions, beliefs we take for granted. Justifiable assumptions lead to reasonable inferences. Assumptions often operate at the unconscious level. When we uncover our assumptions, we often find the roots of prejudice, stereotyping, bias, and other forms of irrational thinking.

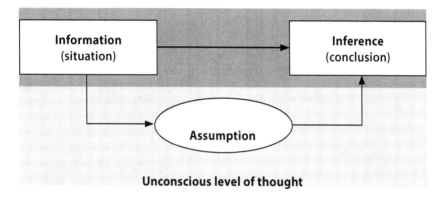

Consider these examples:

Situation: Your nation is in a conflict with another nation.

Inference: Your nation is justified in this conflict.

Assumption: Your nation is always justified in its conflicts with other nations.

Situation: I got an "A" in my composition class.

Inference: That proves I am a good writer.

Assumption: All students who get an "A" in composition class are good writers.

Be aware: Inferences follow from assumptions. If our assumptions are faulty, our inferences will be as well.

Consider the following method for identifying inferences and assumptions in one's thinking. We first determine what one might infer (either rationally or irrationally) in a situation. We then figure out the generalization that led to that inference. This is the assumption.

Information (situation)	Possible **Inference** One Might Make	**Assumption** Leading to the Inference
1. You have difficulty learning in class.	1. It is the teacher's fault	1. Whenever students have difficulty learning, it is the teacher's fault.
2. You notice a man reading a book by Karl Marx.	2. The man must be a communist.	2. All people who read books by Karl Marx are communists.
3. You see a child crying next to her mother in the grocery store.	3. The mother has refused to get the child something she wants.	3. Whenever a child is crying next to her mother in the grocery store, the mother has refused to give the child something she wants.
4. You see a man sitting on a curb with a paper bag in his hand.	4. The man must be a bum.	4. All men sitting on curbs with paper bags in their hands are bums.

Now think up your own situations. Formulate inferences that might follow from those situations. Then figure out the assumption that led to each inference.

Situation	Possible **Inference** One Might Make	**Assumption** Leading to the Inference
1.		
2.		
3.		
4.		

Conclusion

Clearly there are many varieties of analysis specific to particular disciplines and technical practices. These forms of analysis often require technical training of a specialized nature. For example, one cannot do qualitative analysis in chemistry without instruction in chemistry.

What we have provided in this guide, however, is the common denominator between all forms of analysis because all forms require thoughtful application and all thought presupposes the elements of thought. For example, one cannot think analytically FOR NO PURPOSE. Or think analytically, with NO QUESTION in mind. This much should be self-evident. Unfortunately, it is not self-evident to most students.

Those who would develop analytic minds need guidance, instruction, and practice in monitoring their thinking using intellectual tools applicable to every discipline. They need to learn to question purposes, goals, problem definitions, information, concepts, etc… It is these interdisciplinary analytic tools that enable those skilled in them to understand and assess their analytic thinking, whether in a highly technical area or in an everyday personal application. It is these analytic tools that enable one to get at the most fundamental logic of any discipline, subject, problem, or issue. They provide the means for transfer of learning between and among subjects and disciplines. They enable motivated persons to gain an overview of their learning in any and every situation analyzed, to think their way into and out of various intellectual domains.

Of course, there are no magic pills that will create analytic questioning minds. As in any important area of skills and abilities, all learners need to log hundreds of hours to gain command and deep insight. There are no shortcuts. We hope that this thinker's guide will serve as a launching pad toward analytic proficiency. It is admittedly a first step only, but it is an essential, and we believe a powerful, first step. The question is, "Do you have the will and the insight to commit yourself to the long-term practice required?"

The Thinker's Guide Library provides convenient, inexpensive, portable references that students and faculty can use to improve the quality of studying, learning, and teaching. Their modest cost enables instructors to require them of all students (in addition to a textbook). Their compactness enables students to keep them at hand whenever they are working in or out of class. Their succinctness serves as a continual reminder of the most basic principles of critical thinking. (Also available in ebook format.)

For Students & Faculty

 Critical Thinking—The essence of critical thinking concepts and tools distilled into a 24-page pocket-size guide. **#520m**

 Analytic Thinking—This guide focuses on the intellectual skills that enable one to analyze anything one might think about — questions, problems, disciplines, subjects, etc. It provides the common denominator among all forms of analysis. **#595m**

 Asking Essential Questions—Introduces the art of asking essential questions. It is best used in conjunction with the Miniature Guide to Critical Thinking and the Thinker's Guide on How to Study and Learn. **#580m**

 How to Study & Learn—A variety of strategies—both simple and complex—for becoming not just a better student, but also a master student. **#530m**

 How to Read a Paragraph—This guide provides theory and activities necessary for deep comprehension. Imminently practical for students. **#525m**

 How to Write a Paragraph—Focuses on the art of substantive writing. How to say something worth saying about something worth saying something about. **#535m**

 The Human Mind—Designed to give the reader insight into the basic functions of the human mind and how knowledge of these functions (and their interrelations) can enable one to use one's intellect and emotions more effectively. **#570m**

 Foundations of Ethical Reasoning—Provides insights into the nature of ethical reasoning, why it is so often flawed, and how to avoid those flaws. It lays out the function of ethics, its main impediments, and its social counterfeits. **#585m**

 How to Detect Media Bias and Propaganda—Helps readers recognize bias and propaganda in the daily news so they can reasonably determine what media messages need to be supplemented, counter-balanced, or thrown out entirely. Focuses on the logic of the news and societal influences on the media. **#575m**

 Scientific Thinking—The essence of scientific thinking concepts and tools. It focuses on the intellectual skills inherent in the well-cultivated scientific thinker. **#590m**

 Fallacies: The Art of Mental Trickery and Manipulation—Introduces the concept of fallacies and details 44 foul ways to win an argument. **#533m**

For Students & Faculty, cont.

 Engineering Reasoning—Contains the essence of engineering reasoning concepts and tools. For faculty it provides a shared concept and vocabulary. For students it is a thinking supplement to any textbook for any engineering course. **#573m**

 Glossary of Critical Thinking Terms & Concepts—Offers a compendium of more than 170 critical thinking terms for faculty and students. **#534m**

 Aspiring Thinker's Guide to Critical Thinking—Introduces critical thinking using simplified language (and colorful visuals) for students. It also contains practical instructional strategies for fostering critical thinking. **#554m**

 Clinical Reasoning—Introduces the clinician or clinical student to the foundations of critical thinking (primarily focusing on the analysis and assessment of thought), and offers examples of their application to the field. **#564m**

 Critical and Creative Thinking—Focuses on the interrelationship between critical and creative thinking through the essential role of both in learning. **#565m**

 Intellectual Standards— Explores the criteria for assessing reasoning; illuminates the importance of meeting intellectual standards in every subject and discipline. **#593m**

 Historical Guide for Students—Focuses on history as a mode of thinking; helps students see that every historical perspective can be analyzed and assessed using the tools of critical thinking; develops historical reasoning abilities **#584m**

For Faculty

 Active and Cooperative Learning—Provides 27 simple ideas for the improvement of instruction. It lays the foundation for the ideas found in the guide *How to Improve Student Learning*. **#550m**

 Critical Thinking Competency Standards— Provides a framework for assessing students' critical thinking abilities. **#555m**

 Critical Thinking Reading and Writing Test—Assesses the ability of students to use reading and writing as tools for acquiring knowledge. Provides grading rubrics and outlines five levels of close reading and substantive writing. **#563m**

 Educational Fads— Analyzes and critiques educational trends and fads from a critical thinking perspective, providing the essential idea of each one, its proper educational use, and its likely misuse. **#583m**

  How to Improve Student Learning—Provides 30 practical ideas for the improvement of instruction based on critical thinking concepts and tools. **#560m**

 Socratic Questioning—Focuses on the mechanics of Socratic dialogue, on the conceptual tools that critical thinking brings to Socratic dialogue, and on the importance of questioning in cultivating the disciplined mind. **#553m**

 Historical Guide for Instructors—Focuses on history as a mode of thinking; offers instructors critical thinking tools to use in the classroom. Provides rubrics for assessing student work. **#586m**